The World According to

Rex Felixx

Volume: 1

By: Rex Felixx

Keep dreaming,

and creating a better tomorrow.

Don't let your head

deter you from what

your heart really needs.

RF

To Craw,

forever my rock.

Connected.

The world is dark.

The world is wild.

Empty places,

with a sea full of faces.

So alone...

yet we are

So connected.

Everyone checks in :

statuses,

locations,

pictures,

Depicting a life.

A life,

that we all dream of...

but then we

realize,

that we quit

dreaming years ago.

RF

OODLE! POODLE!

OODLE! POODLE! KADOODLE!
I HAD A POODLE.
WHO ATE TOO MANY NOODIES
NOW HE'S FAT!
AND I'M SAD.

CHEWINGUM IS HARD.

I WANNA CHEW SOME GUM.
BUT I'M A LAZY BUM.
I DON'T WANNA GO TO THE STORE.
I'D RATHER SIT HERE AND ROAR!

No more.

No more negative.

No more hate.

No more saltiness.

No more comfortable life.

No more failures.

No more.

RF

New Day

A new day

and fresh starts.

Rise up from your anxious slumber.

Adventure out today.

Seize the moments

and don't dwell on the past.

RF

Reality

Back to reality

Fresh new day

Restart.

No more daily grinding it out

to survive.

Time to focus.

Time to live my life

and thrive.

RF

A MOO-MOO STORY.

THERE ONCE A MAN WITH A HAT.
OR WAS IT A BAT?
WHATEVER HE HAD, IT WAS FAT.
I'M NO GOOD AT REMEMBERING STORIES
AND IF I DO, THEY'RE RATHER BORING.
ANYWAYS, THE MAN IN THE HAT
WALKED DOWN THE STREET
LOOKING FOR SOME RAW MEAT.
JUST THEN MY HEART SKIPPED A BEAT
FOR I'M A BIG OL' COW WITH FOUR FEET.
THIS MAN IS HUNGRY, AND WANTS TO EAT.
MOST LIKELY A JUICY STEAK
PROBABLY A SANDWICH HE WILL MAKE.
NOT ME I'M AFRAID
NOT TODAY.
SO I GRABBED MY HOOVES
AND GALLOPED AWAY.

Mundane

Mondays should

be called Mundanes.

Same cycle every week.

Wake up.

Drink coffee,

commute in traffic.

Work .

Sleep.

Repeat.

RF

Tree

Twisted Trunk

with roots in the sand.

How will you stand?

Buried in the shallow ground.

Impoverished tree.

Lonely.

Soon a Widow-Maker to be.

RF

HAM IN HAM.
HAND IN HAND
ARM IN ARM.
I DONNO... SOMETHING LIKE THAT.
I ♥ HAM.

Awake!

Awake oh sleepy giant!

Arise, and do great things.

For soon enough,

those loud judging voices

will soon become

distant echoes.

RF

Simpler Times

Remember holding hands

and all we thought about

was what will happen next?

Short sightedness.

Emotions were fiery and real.

Nothing else mattered,

except that special moment.

Frozen in time.

No money, no problem.

Never any worries,

except how much gas we had left in the tank.

RF

Negative Minds

Negative minds

are only

jaded and confused.

Always be positive

and help those people's lives.

RF

Shadows

We are so afraid

of our own shadows.

If only we looked behind us,

we would see that

it is only the sun shining down from the sky.

Then the whole world would be a much better place.

RF

Wonder

Let them wonder

and wonder,

about what you are doing,

and the places you are headed.

RF

Lost?

Maybe it feels off

maybe we feel awkward,

and feel out of place.

Things never seem to go our way.

Does it mean we are lost?

NO.

We just haven't figured it out yet.

RF

Dinosaur with a Monocle

GOOD DAY SIR

A DINOSAUR WITH A MONOCLE
IS NOT REAL THEY SAY

BUT I SAW ONE ON THE TELLY
JUST THE OTHER DAY.

HE ATE SOME BISCUITS
AND HAD SOME TEA.
OH I WISH! OH I WISH!
ONE DAY HE WILL COME
VISIT ME!

Blaze

What once started

as a delicate ember glowing,

has now exploded

into a whirlwind of

passion and excitement!

Never ending blaze!

For as long

as we both shall live.

RF

Sharks with facial hair.

After the Storm

After the storm,

the sun will come.

After every wicked act,

goodness will overcome.

RF

..98..99...100. Ready or
not here I Come!

Silly me,

I forgot to complain today.

RF

Tomorrow

Rest this evening,

for tomorrow,

a new day begins,

and will never wait.

RF

The Lonely Flower

The lonely flower

sits high among the weeds.

Her bloom is everlasting,

while the rest vanish and sleep.

All too fast summer is ending,

and fields upon fields

of rainbow colored collections,

wither to the soft earth below.

All but one flower left,

It's the grand finale! The final act!

Not one cloud in sight,

to cover her radiant beauty.

But in the end, there is no escape,

from the wintery winds that will howl and quake.

Farewell my love,

until next season,

when we shall both meet again.

RF

This Life

This world we live in

makes no sense.

Hypocrite and lies

what was great, is now taboo.

No rules, just destruction .

All I want is to live.

A life for me,

my wife,

and our baby.

In a world,

happy and carefree.

RF

SLEEP

WHILE THE WORLD SLEEPS
I LAY AWAKE.
BLANK STARE
COUNTING MY CARES.
CONVERSATIONS WITH MY THOUGHTS
WHILE THE SHADOWS OF THE MOON WALK.
WHAT IS A THOUGHT?
WHAT IS A DREAM?
JUST A FEW THINGS
TO PONDER,
FROM THE MAN WHO CAN'T SLEEP.

Woke up today,
feeling no pressure.
Woke up today,
feeling brand new.
Woke up today,
wiser than my years.
Woke up today,
and going to face my fears.

RF

Spark

Groggy and tired

need a spark or a fire.

Something to awaken my senses

and lead me to my dreams and desires.

One little spark,

to warm me up so I can finally start.

RF

Walter the Cat

Walter the Cat

Has no friends.

However,

he has finally made amends

with this ol' rat.

Funny to think,

a cat...

and a rat...

acquaintances...

Just imagine that.

RF

Ash and Bones

Blood and bones

is how we are born.

Ash and dirt is what we will become.

Somewhere in between

is where we decide how to be loved and formed.

RF

Morning Silence

Silence sings their song.

All quiet this early morn.

Sometimes the hush-hush,

is where we should start.

Minus the beating of our hopeful heart.

RF

THE WORLD IS HARD,
KEEP ON MOVING.
DON'T STOP!
DON'T GIVE UP!
KEEP ON BREATHING,
KEEP ON TRYING.

-RF-

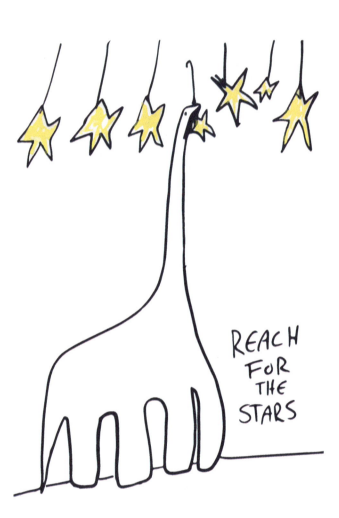

More time

I just need more time...

So I can waste it,

like I did with

my younger years.

RF

Love with your whole self.
Love without fear.
Love with no remorse.
Love always
Love you forever.

RF

Foggy
Rainy
Cold
Wet
   Days.

Make
Me
So
Tired
And
 Make
Me
 Want
  TO
 SLEEP
On
 The
SOFA
All
  Day!

RF

THE LONELY CART.

All alone
in this sea of asphalt.
Crowds of strangers
avoid eye contact,
no relief,
no inner peace,
I just want to be
reunited
with my metal family.
Please!
Oh please!!
someone help me.
Lonely cart I have become,
but don't allow me
to be vindictive
towards my previous owner
who abandoned me.
I'm not angry or upset,
I just want a tiny, tiny breeze
to set me free, into the next
SUV that I see.

RP

Today

Today's the day

where I won't be afraid.

Today's the day,

when I will live my dreams all day.

Today's the day...

" Oh look something shiny!"

RF

Dinosaurs and Donuts

Dinosaurs and donuts

go together like

toothpaste and orange juice.

A dinosaur wouldn't eat a donut.

Only us "advanced people "enjoy dehydrated flour,

and high fructose corn syrup jam.

RF

Beware!

Beware of the traps and snares

of the dreaded naysayer.

Quick to say "No",

before they ever "know."

Criticizing sneers,

as they chatter with your peers.

Sleight of hand, comfortably smug.

Mocking your highest potential,

while you strive for dreams of success and of far away lands.

But as they slumber,

alone in their cave of despair,

you keep on climbing until

you reach your goals up there.

RF

Creative Chaos

Creative chaos

in an empty room

full of blank paper,

writing and typing,

drawing and molding,

my lovely creation into existence.

Looking inward

focusing onward,

only I decide

who breathes or who dies.

Create or destroy.

My world, my rules

in this novel story.

RF

Arm to Arm

Hand in Hand,

Arm to arm,

we will travel the world,

and go through all the land.

Exciting things so see

and interesting people to greet.

So many years ahead

to go where you wanna go,

and be who you wanna be.

RF

We've had so many awful days this year.

Make tomorrow something special.

SOMETHING AWESOME!

RF

Adulthood

Days turn

into

months

into

years.

Seems like everything around me changes.

Except for me.

Punching in,

Punching out.

The only constant is

this immovable force

called adulting throughout.

RF

Who am I.

I am strong
I am awesome
I can talk to everyone.
I laugh
I make people laugh
I am smart
I am a Husband
I am a best friend
I am kind
I am gentle
I am funny
I am weird
I can create
I have a voice
I sing loud
I draw well
I am me
But who are you?

I have this little boil,

He won't leave me be.

He always tries to foil,

my date I had from last Saturday eve.

This girl loved me more than dirt and soil.

Until she saw this big bag of oil.

Now good old rosy cheeked Cheryl

left me for some

brute name "Dirty Thirty" Earl.

RF

Heart and String

Connected by love

Two hearts become one.

Memories and history

seamlessly sewn in place,

like a royal tapestry,

intricately stitched forever in this time and space.

RF

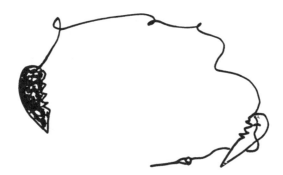

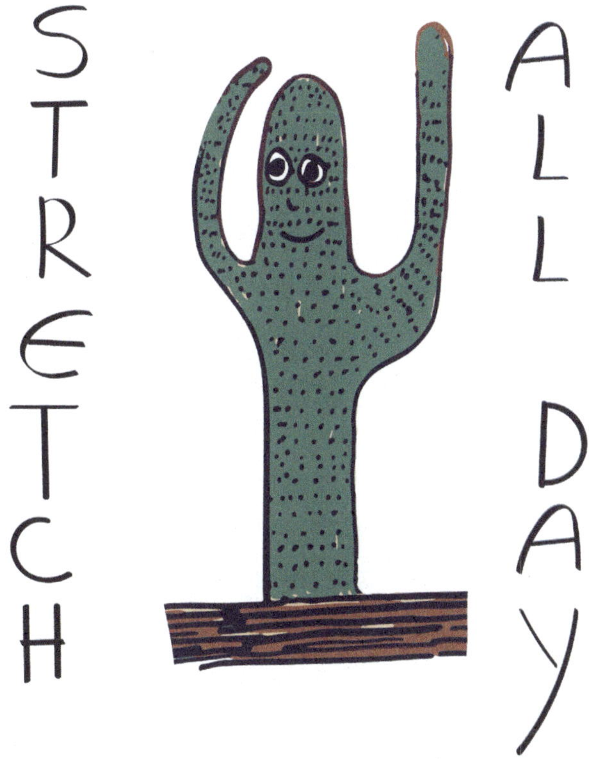
STRETCH
ALL DAY

Old and Gray

I don't wanna

be old and gray,

watching my time pass,

as my slowly bones decay.

Sitting on a lazy-boy,

and watching the dreadful news each day.

I want to sing, laugh, jump, and dance,

before my final resting day!

Most importantly,

be unapologetically free,

and forget what the world

and what others may say about me.

I am always youthful,

but never old and gray.

RF

Wheel Life

Round and round we go,

like gerbils on a wheel,

sprinting for hours on end,

spinning until we are in a tizzy.

Round and round we go,

like gerbils on a wheel,

sprinting for hours on end,

spinning until we are in a tizzy.

Round and round we go,

like gerbils on a wheel,

sprinting for hours on end,

spinning until we are in a tizzy.

Round and round we go,

like gerbils on a wheel,

sprinting for hours on end,

spinning until we are in a tizzy.

RF

Social Media

Social media

silences the masses

removes human emotions by using likes and clicks.

Reduces our vocabulary to

LOLS and BRB.

RF

Streetcar Navigation

Streetcar

take me away

through the city

and out to the country

where I can live and breathe

without the toxicity.

RF

Somewhere, Someplace

Somewhere, Someplace

There is someone waiting for you.

One day you will meet.

Oh what a joy,

What a grand day that will be!

However,

until that moment arrives,

appreciate yourself,

and love the simple joys.

RF

It Happens

Life happens

Love happens

We happen

It happens

Failure happens

Awful happens

Liking happens

Temptation Happens

Annoyance Happens

Together Happens

Emotion Happens

Joy Happens

Age Happens

Screwing Up Happens

Struggle Happens

Sickness happens

RF

Sit and rest

Relax and unwind

The world will keep moving

whether you want it to or not.

Let the earth spin,

sit back and see what happens next.

RF

The Ghoul Twins

The ghoul twins

all fought and sought

for the love of their mother.

Johnny was the golden ghoul,

while Jimmy was the golden fool.

Mother exclaimed with a cry,

"Be more like him,

and not yourself foolish Jim."

Then with a face so grim,

Jimmy got up and floated away,

and he is still lost

to this very, very, day.

RF

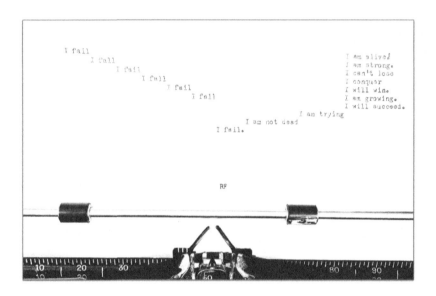

Laugh forever

Laugh so hard your sides hurt.

Surround yourself with the peers you adore,

so the sadness isn't a cloud above.

Remember, cookie cutter people are awful ,

and have no sense

of the humor that we possess.

RF

I ENJOY LIFE,
I LOVE MY WIFE.
I EVEN EAT APPLE PIE,
WHEN I CLOSE MY ONE EYE.

I LOVE...

LIFE.

Little Star

Little star

high above

alone by day,

smothered by night.

In the crowded night sky,

I've lost you

little one.

Keep shining bright,

and everything will

always turn out alright.

RF

Disguises

Beware of masked people.

They smile one moment,

and the next,

backstab you,

to make them feel more relevant.

Your disguises may fool so many people,

but you won't fool me.

RF

Never

Keep trying

Your face may be in the gutter,

bruised and broken,

but don't give up.

NEVER GIVE UP.

RF

Be Gone

Negative self thought,

BE GONE.

Worrisome mentality,

BE GONE.

Anxiety brain drain,

BE GONE.

Successful, joyous thoughts,

BE HERE!

RF

Ducks rough day.

Mr. Duck

was down on his luck.

Not one thing went right.

For that cold day was such a fight.

Someone stole his favorite truck,

and farmer John gave him a good hard pluck.

He tripped on his shoes,

which gave him a big black bruise.

His tiny back hurt,

and then he snagged and ripped his favorite green shirt.

Nothing went his way

on that cold November day.

Then late that night

as he rest in bed,

he thought:

"tomorrow will be better,"

as he smirked, and laid down his weary head.

RF

Window

From my window,

I can see the rustling of the trees from the cool breeze.

From my window,

I can day dream of far off worlds.

From my window,

I can feel no pain.

From my window,

I have my own world,

where no one but me

can rule this space.

RF

Insomnia

Lying awake

in this groggy world.

Lost and confused.

Tossing and turning on these annoying box springs,

putting on a show

for the white walls and alarm clock to see.

RF

Go on

See that mountain,

Go and conquer it.

See that dream,

Go on achieve it to make it a reality.

You see that beef and bean burrito,

Go on and devour it.

RF

You can do great things

Just believe in yourself.

RF

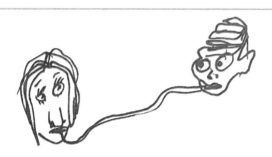

```
Yammy Tammy
 Clammy hands
after she was holding Richard  Pritchard's
hands in the bandstand.
Holly, Jolly,
the music played
until the wires frayed,
and the music strayed off.
Luckily, Yammy Tammy's hands
were held tight so they could exit the venue
before the wire fire ensue.
They ran into a girl named Lily Ann Sue,
who cooked great food,
which made them get in the mood
for some homemade noodles kaboodles
 at Lily Ann Sue's place.
It's not a huge space,
rather small,
but the crew went and had a joyous ball.
As they sat and sang "Noodles kaboodles rule
my patoodle strudel moodle!" in the food hall!

                RF
```

Remember

Don't let uncertainty

paralyze your life.

Keep living,

Keep dreaming,

Remember who you are.

RF

Listen

Listen closely

to that thumping going on in your heart.

It will tell you when to move on,

or when to finally go on and start.

RF

Fools

Nothing wrong

with acting like a fool.

Even when others

are way too cool.

Don't lose your spark,

always stay being true.

RF

Candle

Like a candle

perched on the nightstand.

I will eventually

flicker and sway

until the wax melts,

and I will slowly fade away.

RF

I love my life!

Even when it kicks

my teeth in.

RF

Circles

Running around

going nowhere.

Start or finish

it's actually the same.

Is it just me?

Or am I going insane?

RF

Living Life

Travel the world.

Speak your mind.

Learn that hobby.

Tell them that you love them.

And remember,

live for today,

because we never know

what tomorrow may bring.

RF

Keep

Keep dreaming.

Keep doing.

Keep breathing.

Keep growing.

RF

Storytime

Everyday comes,

and every evening goes.

Doesn't mean the story ends,

just a new chapter unfolds.

RF

Alone

Sometimes being alone

is the remedy

that every person needs.

RF

Knock, Knock

Knock, Knock

uncertainty knocks

twice upon my door.

While the wind keeps blowing

and streetlights glowing.

Tap...

Tap...

No one is here,

leave me be.

I don't want to face

this future of uncertainty.

RF

Thoughts on broccoli:

It's green and I don't like it.

thank you.

RF

Paths

Different paths

where we all wander.

Some of us sprint,

while others walk and ponder.

Some are fast,

and inevitably crash.

Some are slow,

causing delays and cramps.

Life isn't a race,

so go at your own pace,

as long as you continue

to learn and grow

each and everyday.

RF

Youth/ Old

The younger we are,

the more giggles we have.

The more ancient we are,

the more cynical we become.

RF

Chirping With Crows

THERE WAS A CROW NAMED JOHN LEON

HE HAS NO PLACE TO CALL HIS OWN

BUT TOWN TO TOWN HE ALWAYS FLOCKS

AND ALL THE NEIGHBORS DON'T GIVE A CROCK

BECAUSE JOHN LEON IS A BIRD

AND ANYONE THAT CARES IS JUST ABSURD

FRANCIS
        THE FLYING PHEASANT

FRANCIS THE PHEASANT
WANTED TO FLY

So HE BOUGHT A JETPACK
FOR LORD KNOWS WHY.

HE TOLD HIS PARENTS YESTERDAY
THEY SCREAMED AND BEGAN TO CRY.

MOTHER STATED-
"A PHEASANT SHOULD WALK,
AND NEVER FLY."

FRANCIS RESPONDED-
"MOTHER YOU ARE WRONG,
YOU WILL SEE ME TOMORROW FLOAT ON BY."

HE LOADED UP HIS PACK WITH ESSENTIALS
YOYO'S, CRAYONS, AND HIS TEDDY NAMED "FRENCH FRY"

THE COUNTDOWN BEGAN
NO ONE WATCHED, FOR THEY SURELY KNEW HE'D DIE.

ALL HIS LIFE, FRANCIS THE PHEASANT
WANTED TO FLY.

UP AND UP AND UP HE WENT,
ZIPPING THROUGH THE CLOUDS, HIGH IN THE SKY!

HO HUM.   HO HUM.

HO HUM
I SIT ON MY BUM
         AND WATCH THE WORLD GO BY.

HO HUM
ME AND MY CHUMS
         RATHER SIT INSIDE
            THAN PLAY OUTSIDE.

WE STARE AND GLARE
AT THE WORLD OUT THERE
BUT DECIDE
         WE ARE BETTER OFF ALONE
      WITH OUR SCREEN ON OUR PHONE.

Puddle Jumping

Running,

Jumping,

Skipping,

Never any worries.

Puddle splashing

was all we cared about.

Childhood memories,

oh so innocent.

We could do anything

without any doubts.

RF

Retired Pirate

I'm fully retired now.

I've done my fair share,

I travelled the world,

and dated all the gals.

However,

my favorite parrot pal is gone.

All me gold is lost.

I drank way more

then I ever could think.

Alas,

I sit on my bum,

and keep rapidly drinking more and more rum.

Hoping to join that next high seas adventure.

Help me to pay for my tavern tab,

and to tell my stories

to all the new pirate lads.

RF

SITTING

Sitting and waiting,

wishing and hoping,

for the sun to rise,

and the moon to finally set.

Longing for the warmth to come

and for the icy chill to erase.

RF

The Wind Waltz

The trees bow and bend,

synchronized in song.

A waltz,

A courtship,

under silver lined skies.

RF

Together

We can do anything

Stand tall,

don't back down.

Conquer those fears,

and break your chains.

Never alone in this fight,

but together through the night.

RF

Steps

One step forward

Three steps back

Sometimes in circles,

sometimes backtrack.

High and low,

fast or slow,

where we end up

God only knows.

RF

BUBBLE LIFE.

I LIVE IN THIS BUBBLE
SO I DON'T CAUSE NO TROUBLE
AND SO NO TROUBLE BOTHERS ME.
I WISH I COULD RIDE A BIKE,
BUT NO ROOM IN HERE
EXCEPT FOR THIS LIL TIKE.
NO FRIENDS, NO PAIN.
NO SHAME, NO FAME.
ME MYSELF AND I
ALL ALONE,
IN MY TINY BUBBLE
BUBBLE, FULL OP NO TROUBLE.

Libations and Emotions

Drink the poison

let it burn down.

Swallow it quickly

before you get ill.

Tomorrow we will worry,

for tonight we shall be merry.

RF

The Great Swim

I want to swim

from Kentucky to London,

with no one but my grin.

No one said it was a good idea

but they are jealous of me

and my soon to be famous swim.

I jumped in from Kentucky

and out to the sea.

I never made it past San Luis Dupree.

I got a cramp

and had to turn back.

So then I quit,

and went back to sleep.

RF

Never Try, Never Fail.

If you never try,

then you will never fail.

No one will never know your name.

Now this doesn't mean fame,

for they surely are not the same.

Deep down inside all of our hearts

we have a purpose.

It's always been there

right from the very start.

RF

Tacos & Salsa

Tacos and Salsa

no cheese or jalapeños

just sour cream

and hard corn shell.

P.S. No Tomato!

If you would please.

RF

Evenings

Carefree life.

While we are here,

no worries or strife.

Under the moonlit sky

and warm embers at our feet,

evenings like these are impossible to beat.

RF

Wanderer

We are all searching

looking for the truth.

Wandering to find a place

where we feel wanted.

A place to call home.

RF

Wit and Spit

Wit and Spit

without them both

we have no grit.

Without them both,

we cannot successfully navigate

through our so called life.

RF

Stale Toast

I need to know

where to travel,

and where to go.

Treading water.

Stale toast on the counter.

Up a creek without a paddle.

I need to know

which way to go ,

to live my life

and to continue to grow.

RF

Mornings

Wet feet,

from the morning dew.

The sun rises

far over the tops of the evergreens.

Eight a.m.

the lawn mowers are already revving.

Spring has sprung.

The Winter decay is finally done.

RF

Punching In

7 am. The day begins

12 pm. lunchtime again (ham and Swiss)

3 pm. Afternoon coffee splash with a little cream dash.

4 pm. Day over.

7am. Let's do it again.

7am. Let's do it again

7 am. Let's ...

.

Sing

Make noise

Loud and proud

Scream until your lungs give out

Release the stress

Unleash your inner wind

Dig deep,

and truly be alive from within.

Rest Your Soul

Rest.

Refresh your soul

in the green meadow and morning dew.

Rays of light pierce the monochromatic clouds.

Songbirds and bees

bring forth the songs of the trees.

Strengthen your purpose

in the silence of creation.

RF

Springtime

Rain sprinkles down from the sky

Drip, drop.

Drip, drop.

Down, down, down

upon my face.

Baptize my mind

and make me feel alive

on this very day.

RF

I FEEL LOST....

SOMETIMES

AWKWARD UMBRELLA MOMENTS.

DON'T
GIVE
UP
HOMIE !

-RF-

- EGG SOLILOQUY -

I'M AN EGG
I'VE GOT NO LEGS.
I'VE NEVER TRAVELLED,
ONLY BEEN SCRAMBLED.
SO LITTLE TO DO
JUST STAND HERE,
I MEAN LAY HERE
WAITING FOR SOMEONES
FORK TO SQUISH MY
YOLKY BRAIN.
  — RF

Elephants Do Swim

SWIM LITTLE ELEPHANT, SWIM.
THE SUN'S SETTING AND IT'S GETTING DIM.
THERE'S NOT MUCH HOPE,
EVEN AFTER CAPTAIN PAT THREW YOU A ROPE.
HURRY LITTLE ONE, THE SHARKS ARE CIRCLING
AND IT'S GETTING GRIM.
WELL DON'T BE MAD AT ME.
I DIDN'T PUSH YOU IN.
THAT WAS A CRAZY FAT PORCUPINE,
NAMED RIVERBOAT JIM.

Warranties

When I was young,

I thought by this time in the future,

I'd have a fancy flying jetpack,

and a favorite vacation spot called Jurassic Park!

Instead,

My bones always ache when I awake,

and I have approximately 3500 robo-calls

about my 2008 Ford Escape Warranty.

P.S. Never Have I ever had a Ford Escape.

RF

Doubts

I always have my doubts

I always have my cloudy thoughts

But I always try,

And that gives me hope.

RF

Face

I remember that face

I will never forget that day.

You were always beautiful,

like a songbirds song,

or the sunrise on a warm summer's day.

RF

Friends

Lifelong

summertime fun

clapping around

singing some songs.

Enjoying that cool night breeze.

Destress.

Mind is always at ease,

When you have friends

that you don't have to please.

RF

Sun

What a lovely day

for positive thoughts

and soaking up the Sun's rays.

RF

Feet Meet Nature.

Wet leaves beneath my feet.

Silent steps upon the grass,

cuffed pants begin to wet,

from the dew on the blades of green.

No place to go,

no place to be,

just me and my feet

and the nature we greet.

RF

COOKIE CUTTER

Cookie cutter people

Cardboard cutouts, fake people, and phonies.

We are them,

we all were them,

we all strive to be them.

Boring, dull, exasperating!

Striving to be perfect cutouts of people who are nobody.

RF

A Fish Bowl Thought

A fish

in a tank

longing for some freedom.

Tail to nose,

touching end to end.

No room to grow,

just confined to this small fish bowl.

RF

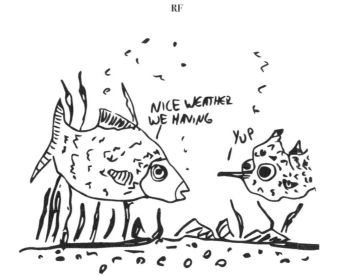

Hang on.

Whatever you are going through.

Hang on.

Hold on.

It may not always get easier,

but it will eventually get better.

TRUST ME.

RF

Jitters

Hearts pumping

Head isn't thinking

My words are jumbled

Tongue tied beyond belief.

Thump! Thump! Thump!

Like a drum,

beating faster, and faster.

Butterflies and nausea,

all while my eyes remain connected to yours.

"Hello."

"Hi."

RF

ARTIE THE ANTEATER

Mister Anteater

why do you eat so much?

Now you have a hairy gut,

and are in a troublesome rut.

You spoiled your appetite

after that very last bite.

Too many tiny ants ,

makes it hard

to fit into those overall style pants.

RF

FICKLE PICKLE

A fickle pickle

ran down the street

with nothing but his bowler hat

and an alleyway cat named Chester E. Bat.

laughing and chuckles,

leather shoes with brass buckles

as he clattered along the way.

everyone smiled and laughed

at this fickle pickle

who decided to get up and run away.

RF

Tiny Seed

One tiny seed

can become a giant oak tree.

One tiny dream

can become your reality.

RF

Through It All

Through it all,

I will stand tall.

No sleet

No winds

No fire

No rain

No hail

No typhoons

will ever make me fall.

RF

#SOCIAL

London Bridge

London Bridge

may have fallen,

and Rome may have burned,

but my love for you will never fade away to black.

RF

Dawn

By dawn's early light

I can see your restful smile.

The world may be burning,

but can't we just lay

here for a little while?

RF

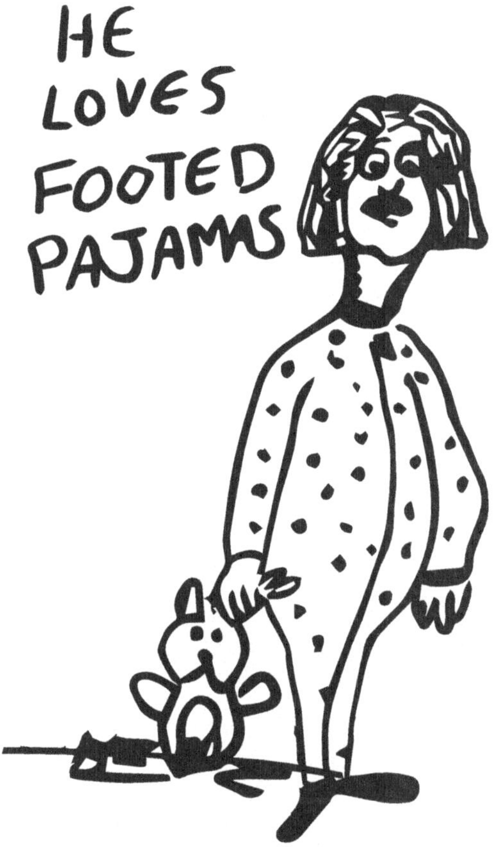
HE
LOVES
FOOTED
PAJAMS

Shadows

Stay strong,

don't be afraid

of the shadows at night.

You have the light inside you,

to turn the shadows bright.

RF

PIGGY
IN
SAFE ZONE.

An Open Book

Dust me off,

open me up,

read every page.

Every single page.

No secrets,

nothing is hidden from your view.

Chapter by chapter

Hour by hour.

Time stands still,

all of this feels surreal.

Just us two

sitting here.

Just you and me

and me and you.

RF

Darkness.

Be still,

my aching heart.

A new day always will come.

This midnight twilight is only temporary.

RF

"SHEEP SWEARS"

Hills and Valleys

Highs and lows

Hills and valleys.

That's life my friend.

Hold those most dearest to you

closest to you.

Never let go,

of those you love most.

RF

I'm sinking
Help!
SANDY Cheeks
HeRE I come.

I'M A PRICKly
LIL GUY
I WANNA BE FRIENDS
BUT CAREFUL
ON MY BIRTHDAY.
SEND ME NO BALLOONS
FOR THEY WILL DIE
CUZ I'M A LIL PRICKly GUY.

THIS FEELS
SO GRAND.

WITH THE WORLD GONE,

AND NOTHING BUT ME

AND MY HEAD IN THE SAND.

RF -

ALEXANDER
BIRD ESQ

I HAVE A BIRD IN MY BRAIN
IT'S REALLY A DRAIN.
FEEDING FOR TWO
PIZZA FOR ME
PIZZA FOR YOU.
DOLLAR HERE
DOLLAR THERE.
NOT REALLY FAIR
SINCE I DO
ALL THE TALKING
AND WALKING
AND EVEN CHALKING.

SINCE I TEACH
GEOMETRY PART-TIME
AT ST MARYS
DOWN THE STREET
NEAR THE BEACH.
BUT THIS BIRD IS NOT FINE
I DRAW THE LINE
TIRED OF THIS MOOCHING BIRD ON MY HEAD
WHERE HE'S MADE A PERMANENT BED.

- RF -

Hope.

This year is almost over.

Close the door,

move on to what is next.

Pandemic and strife

are soon over,

and this gives me hope.

RF

PUDDLE
OF
WOES

MY FEET ARE SOAKED
THIS AIN'T NO JOKE
THE LEFT IS WET
THE OTHER JUST WEPT
NOW BOTH HAVE MET
THE SAME FATE TOGETHER
WHAT TO DO?
WHAT TO DO?
PRUNY TOES
AND SMELLY WOES
MY MOTHER WILL BE MAD
OR SURELY SAD
AT THE BOY
WHO'S MIND GOT MUDDLED
AND DECIDED TO JUMP IN THAT PUDDLE

Hold me

A loving embrace

is all you need to

take the chill away.

RF

Lighthouse

Heart full of love

in a world torn apart.

You are my lighthouse

when I'm lost in the dark.

The ember of creative thought

when I need a spark.

Forever, together,

right from the start

RF

NED.

Hi, I'm Ned the Turtle.

My favorite color is purple.

All the girls love me,

cuz I have a shell,

and I wax it well.

That's why I have a date tonight.

I hope I do it right.

We are going to Betty's Burger Joint.

I hope she get's the point.

That I am ready ,

to finally go steady!

P.S. I bought her a fluffy teddy.

RF

CRY RHINO CRY.

GO AHEAD AND LAUGH!
LEAVE ME BE.
WHAT DO I CARE
A BIG OL BABY LIKE ME.
I GOTTA PEE!
I GOTTA PEE!
I'M STUCK OUTSIDE
I NEED MORE PRIVACY
WOE IS ME!
A BIG CRYING RHINO
WHO HAS TO PEE!

Always remember ...

We all screw up.

RF

Fail

You can't fail

if you don't even try.

It saddens me

that's how some people

choose to live.

RF

Steps

One little step,

is all you need

to get the motion started,

so you can begin your day.

A herculean effort,

it takes to rise from your slumber.

RF

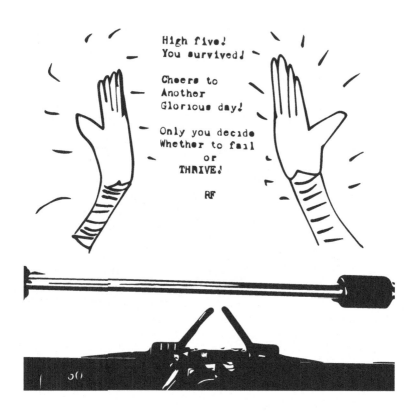

Life begins

life ends

Everything in between

is what we have, friends.

RF

Little Rudy two shoes

Always had the heartache blues.

That girl Jenny never liked him.

Maybe if his name wasn't Rudy, but Jim.

He picked her flowers

but Jenny loved her powers,

and broke his heart every time.

However,

No tooth Susie decided to give him a try.

Rudy smiled and with a cry,

grabbed her hand,

and announced their marriage at the base of the tire swing.

Together they played

for which seemed like hours and hours that day,

Until recess ended,

and their parents took them away.

RF

Paths

Same directions

we all go.

Birth to death

rightfully so.

Left or right,

Dark or bright.

Who even knows?

Where you end up

and where your path finally flows.

RF

Crack that porcelain mask,

BE FREE!

RF

FlOATING ON

I'M DROWNING!
I'M DROWNING!
WILL SOMEONE LEND A HAND?
I KNOW It's NOt HiP
It's NOT COOL
SUCH A BORE
To HELP SOMEONE
IN NEED
INDEED.

YOU EVER
SWIM WITH A POODLE?
While EATING RAMEN NOODLES?
GIVE IT A TRY
GIVE IT A WHIRL

HEN DIAGRAM.

Little

Little by little

we grow each day.

Little by little...

that's all I have to say.

RF

Be Awesome!

Be Extraordinary!

RF

Loved.

You are so loved.

More than my sentences can convey.

You are amazing,

strong and beautiful.

You are the best thing

that has ever happened to me.

RF

Be yourself.

Do what you love,

and love who you are.

Why hold back?

RF

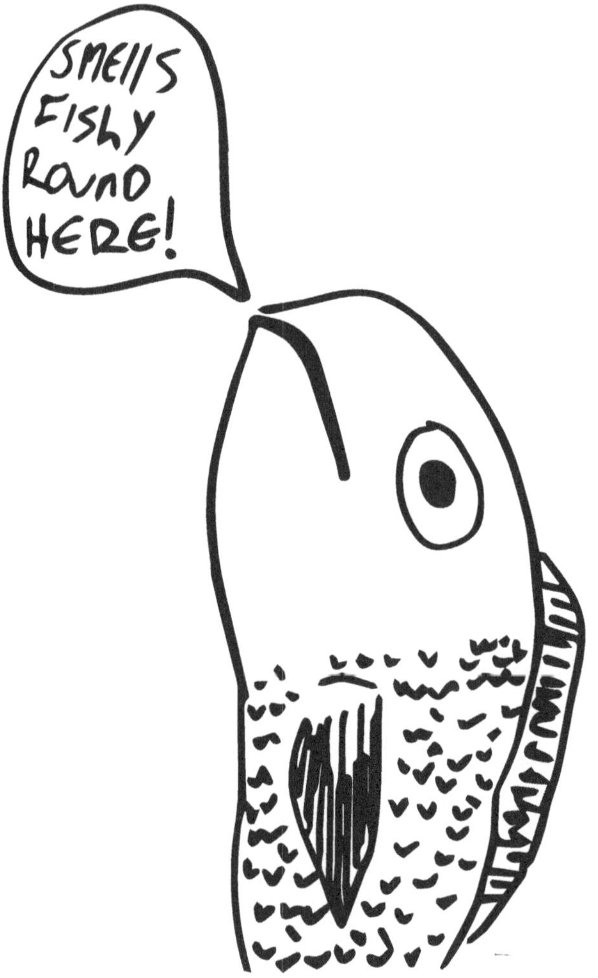
SMELLS FISHY ROUND HERE!

Travel

I travel

not to escape,

but to feel foreign

and to be free.

No nine to five grind.

No gossip of others.

I travel to open

my eyes to the wonderful world I see.

RF

Morning Whispers

I awoke

Not a word was spoke,

as a

glimmer of light danced upon your face.

Love beyond all compare

Filled the air.

Trust, sweet trust,

is all we have,

to live as one.

Rays of light breaks the silence.

Morning turned to day

Day into night.

Every waking moment

with you feels so right.

RF

Roads

I follow the road.

Where it will lead,

God only knows.

, Winding and twisting

millions of stops along the way.

Smiling faces I greet,

while wandering down this dusty, rusty street.

No one can ever take your path.

For it's yours,

and yours alone.

RF

Regrets

Regrets are only a day away.

Enjoy the moments,

live with no fear,

stop making excuses,

and live like you want to stay.

RF

Coast to Coast

I travelled to the coast

searching for who I wanted to be.

When I got there I wasn't

who I was meant to be.

So I picked up the keys

and drove in reverse,

hoping to adjust the ill effects

of who I became,

and hope to mold into something

bigger and better.

RF

Coffee

No sugar,

No cream,

Just black please.

Need all the caffeine,

to get me through this work week.

RF

Endless Wilderness

Time decay

the trees breathe.

Embers heat

and child like awe

round and round we go.

Telling stories of historic lore.

Embers fading,

cool air settles in

darkness engulfs

while we all sleep

under the canopy of the stars

and evergreen trees.

RF

Do things

Do good things

Do memorable good things

Do wonderful memorable good things

RF

10:30

Red lights,

with dancing rain droplets.

10:30 on a Friday night.

Driving to nowhere,

just wasting time.

Damn it feels good

to be so alive.

RF

Moments

Moments come

and moments go.

My feelings for you

I'll never let go.

The crashing waves of emotions,

I'm always drowning in my head.

Should I stay?

Should I go?

Listen to your heart

release yourself,

and let go!

RF

Autumn

The fog slowly rises

as the moon passes,

and the sun rises.

The hooting of the owl

fades away

as the squirrels

come out to play.

All is quiet .

All is fine.

This Autumn season

is so exquisitely divine.

RF

nobody loves
ME!

Love is

Love is never simple

if it is, then it's fake.

Always be true

most especially be you.

For in the end

both hearts are at stake.

RF

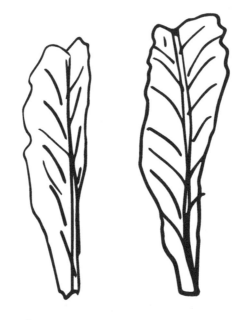

LeHuce BE
    FRIENDS

Embers

As long as the sky

is above,

and the earth is below.

My love for you is the ember that warms and glows.

RF

Frozen Bones

When I'm home alone

the winter winds freeze and chill my bones.

But when I'm with you, I melt away

and the Siberian wolves stay at bay.

Outside,

the icy breeze

and frost gets their way and it's a tundra delight.

Inside our home,

warm and cozy,

our love feels perfectly alright.

RF

Octopus Thinks Too Much

Woe is me.

I have too many arms,

I wanna be free.

I'm so tangled,

in other people's problems.

I'm enwrapped in issues

for which I have no tissues.

Fishes and whales

all annoy me.

Why can't I see?

I need to be me,

use my arms,

not to harm,

but to charm other people's lives.

To create art,

from the heart,

and stop being mean.

For my arms are all I have.

And I need to be the friendliest octopi in the sea.

For whom all the fish, and all the whales

love and hail.

RF

MR CRABBY

MR CRABBY
WHY SO MEAN?
WHY SO RED UHH ANGER?
CHEER UP BE HAPPY
MY LIL CRABBY
SO MUCH LEFT TO BE SEEN.
OUCH! MR CRABBY.
STOP PINCHING ME.
Get OUT OF HERE
YOU ARE FREE!

Don't stare at the sun.

Smiles on T-shirts Aren't Free.

Somedays make me scream.

Working to make a dime.

But all we do is use our time.

Struggle is real

Friends don't know how we often feel.

I need some comfort food

to put me in a good mood.

RF

Wooly Sweater

ME MOTHER
GOT ME THIS
WOOLY SWEATER
I LOVE IT SO
'CEPT ITS TOO LARGE
AND MARGE
TAKES CHARGE
TO INSURE
I KEEP IT ON,
PRISONER ME AM
FOR ME MOTHER
CONTROLS
EVERYTHING
I AM:
FROM SUN UP
TIL SUN DOWN,
ON THE BRIGHTSIDE
ME HAVE THIS
ALL ORGANIC
WOOLY SWEATER.

Absent Mind

Humming a tune,

that I can't explain.

Seeing someone,

and not remembering their name.

Absent minded,

is all part of the game.

RF

Little Cactus

Little Cactus,
Little Cactus,
WHY YoU prick me so?
Ouchie!
Wowchie!
THAT HURT ME BAD.
Now I'M SAD.
OH So SAD!
RF

Keep trying.

Keep going.

Keep breathing.

RF

LOST SHEEP.

PETER THE SHEEP
DON'T GIVE A BLEEP.
HE RAN AWAY TODAY,
HE HOPPED & BOPPED OUT THERE.
MAMA + PAPA SHEEP DON'T KNOW WHERE,
"OH WELL" THEY SAY.
"WE HAVE A HEALTHY STOCK,"
"WE SURELY DON'T GIVE A FLOCK!"

Fly Away

Fly away,

run away with me.

Let's abandon our world

and travel forever and a day.

RF

Blowfish Gonna Blow.

Oh I know

I'm gonna blow!

So much emotion

in this ocean.

I feel so mad,

No make it sad,

about my day today.

Too much stress,

I want much, much less.

Leave me be

so I can sleep

in peace.

I'll take it slow,

Before I go.

For if I don't,

You'll surely know

A fish was here,

before he was blown way out there!

RF

Kites

I flew a kite

just to see

if i might

get away from this place.

No more stress

no more sadness.

Up so high

never going to die.

Just me and my faithful friend.

Truth be told,

I'm too big to fit

in that crazy flying device

it's most likely made

for those tiny tiny mice.

RF

Soaring

There was a time,

when I was afraid to fly.

To spread my wings,

and soar across the bright blue sky.

Then, one day it all clicked.

My eyes were opened

to see all that was important.

To take a leap of faith

and fly high.

Being in the sky is

what it's all about.

Not on the dirty, muddy ground, down and out.

RF

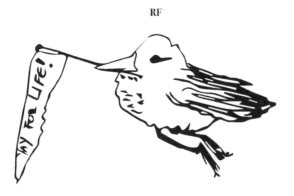

IN MY OWN HEAD
I FOUND A THREAD
I UNRAVELED IT
ROUND AND ROUND IT WENT
TIL I BECAME OLD
AND SPENT.

Little Moments

Enjoy the little moments

each and every day.

In these moments

is where we learn to live and play.

RF

You keep waiting...

and waiting...

and waiting...

Until you miss your moment.

RF

Night Owl

In this twilight,

the peaceful evening

rests in my hands.

Window sill dreaming and

writing while the moon glow beams.

Cloudy thoughts,

and cigar smoke haze.

Sitting,

realizing this evening is **my time** to be alive.

Night owl reflections

darkness awakens my mind.

RF

In a world full of weeds

Be a four leaf clover.

The Sheep

The sheep was on a giant heap

of dirty laundry,

looking for his lost sock.

This sheep was late, oh so late,

for school at 7:30.

"Forget the sock and join the flock."

His mother screamed from across the field.

"I won't be late for goodness sake,

but without this sock I'll surely be mocked from now until eternity."

He galloped out without one sock

and joined his fellow lambs.

Bleating, and screeching the others

pointed and laughed.

With tears held back, he choked

and said "Y'all are horrible , and oh so very mean."

In a snap,

he awoke in his bed, hearing the beeping of an alarm clock.

"Hurry up and join the flock." His mother yelled.

"Oh boy! Oh boy! my sock is clean.

I want to scream! For this horrible day

was all just a dream."

RF

Long and Tall

I have two long legs,

but no hair on top.

I only eat hard boiled eggs,

and drink calorie- free pop.

No one I meet ever smiles.

It's probably because they are in denial.

For I'm the tallest man they ever met,

and they haven't accomplished anything yet.

RF

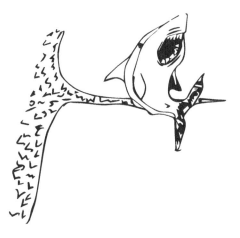

Tree Shark

There once was a shark.

Who lived among the mossy bark.

All the kids would travel and see,

they even named hime Sharky Mcgee.

Everything was great and oh so grand.

Until one Autumn day he got banned.

Poor little Billy O'Houlihan got bit!

In a moments split,

the towns folk agreed

Tree shark Sharky Mcgee

had to be cut down and freed.

RF

Tomorrow

Living and breathing,

doing what you love

not carrying the stress or sorrow.

Let it go,

move on, for today,

is soon tomorrow.

RF

Tangled Laces

Oh bother

my laces are tangled.

How will I ever undo them, from this angle?

Somebody help me please!?

It's too cold out

I don't want to freeze.

RF

Wobble, Wobble

Balance... Balance...

Don't fall down.

Wobble... Wobble...

continue to stay strong

through it all.

RF

Sitting.

Sitting and staring

at the clouds in the sky,

while the tiny ants march on by.

Searching for purpose.

Looking for meaning.

Emerald blades of grass sit patiently

waiting for the drops of dew to evaporate

into the blue atmosphere.

A family of rabbits

hop into my peripheral view,

then in a flash,

gone into the brush.

Out of sight

Out of mind.

Sitting and staring,

wasting time,

as my life flies on by.

RF

Parasites

All around us

sucking us dry.

Taking our energy

until we wither and die.

Can't survive,

without our positive life

that we provide.

Avoid them at all costs

before most of your life is lost.

RF

Trials and Errors

We all have some problems

none of us are perfect,

yet we are all here.

I wish I knew the answers.

I want to be able to help.

Yet I have my own problems to deal with.

RF

Rinse.

Rinse.

Wash.

Repeat.

Daily grind.

Nowhere to be,

nothing to see.

Rinse

Wash.

Repeat.

RF

Shoes

Slip into my shoes

and see what you'll find.

Walking around this earth

with a foggy, cloudy mind.

Step in my footsteps

and see what you'll discover.

So many hidden treasures

left to uncover.

RF

Fiery Arrows

Cradle to grave

a life of happiness

is what I crave.

To have freedom of thought,

to know right from wrong.

Allow me to continue my pursuit of happiness,

without the fiery arrows

piercing me,

and my thoughts,

pinning me to the ground to suffer and rot.

RF

Walls

Stare at wall.

The wall stares back.

Don't talk to a wall,

because the wall doesn't talk back.

RF

Quietly Lost

Lost but not least.

Quietly sitting,

reflecting,

contemplating,

being...

simply being.

RF

Years

Years waiting

Been forever and a day.

Lost at sea

in an ocean of emotion.

Frozen in time

while the world moves by.

No one sees the scars we have

on the inside.

Callous and bruised deep within.

Until that moment,

we finally heard about

YOU.

RF

Deep

Deep down inside you

there is a giant sleeping,

waiting to be awaken.

No more slumber

Make Haste!

Go forth, and seize this day.

RF

Breeze

Soft morning breeze

rustling the purple leaves

in my backyard oasis.

Breathe it in...

Hold...

Breathe it out.

Silence is golden

without a doubt.

RF

Float

We all float on

and rest while we go along.

Flowing along,

nothing can be wrong.

As long as we all

float on...

towards that waterfall

and plunge down, down, down.

Singing this silly silly song.

RF

Do

Do. do. do.

listen to me,

and

Do. Do. Do.

It's all for the greater good.

Don't think for yourself,

just

Do Do Do.

It's all for the greater good.

RF

"TODAY WE ARE WHO WE ARE
WHO KNOWS WHAT TOMORROW
MAY BRING "

RF

Hugs

I need a hug,

not from a bug,

not from a rug,

not from a tortoise,

not from a hare.

I need a hug

from someone I love,

someone who cares.

I need a hug,

I need it quick.

Not tomorrow,

for there is too much sorrow.

Today! Today!

So I can finally say...

I LOVE YOU!!

Now come here

and give me a hug,

ya big lug.

RF

Whiskey thoughts.

Whiskey is so sweet

even after we meet.

Tastes so fine

even when you're already mine.

When you are so far

alone at the bar,

I wish I was there

To drink you up,

and turn my sorrows and frowns

upside down.

RF

Lemming Mind

Like a lemming,

you follow the crowd.

No control.

No remorse.

No recourse to your life.

Path to destruction,

you will be.

The poor old lemming

looking into the mirror,

realizes that the animal looking back

is actually me.

RF

Barbwire

Don't let a few barbwire words

tear your whole world apart.

Keep striving for a purpose

Smile and nod.

RF

Bloom

Flowers bloom

and then decay.

We have finite time

so never delay.

RF

Sunshine

Tan lines

Sun's rays

bring joy

and a

sigh of relief,

that life hasn't ended yet.

And for tomorrow

let's do it

all over again.

RF

September

The leaves will fall

and the chill will soon come.

This doesn't change how I fell

for you, all those seasons ago.

September to remember.

It will come year after year.

My love for you will always be there,

to shelter you from the dreaded frost soon to come.

RF

TRASH.
PANDA.

Where

Heaven

Kisses

Earth,

Is

Where

We

Travel.

RF

I
DROPPED
MY
CROISSANT.

Cope

Goodbyes are the hardest

when you know they won't return.

Life goes on,

even when we are frozen in time.

Each new day,

brings us light and hope.

Memories of our past,

carry us onward.

Until, we can finally

heal and endure

through the rest of this life.

RF

Family

Together we stand

and together we fall.

Build up this family

on solid, solid ground.

RF

ALL WAS SILENT
THEN SUDDENLY
LIKE A PHOENIX BURNING BRIGHT,

YOU RISE FROM THE ASHES,

DETERMINED TO CHANGE YOUR FUTURE

-RF-

REMEMBER
WHO
YOU ARE.

-RF-

EVERYTHING

WILL

BE

OKAY!

RF

Peas And Thank You

Can't we be friends,

and try to make amends?

No more fighting,

just light hearted talking.

Peas in a pod,

i wish we can be.

Forever a family

no fighting indeed.·

RF

Barry the Hairless

Barry! Barry!

Why so scary?

Roaring like a little cubby.

You used to be so hairy.

Barry! Barry!

why so sad?

I know , I know,

Darell shaved you bad.

But be a man

don't get sad ,

Get angry! Get mad!

RF

December Mirage

The winter winds have retreated

and sunshine has been allowed in.

Warmth on my skin

green grass appears again.

Enjoy this mirage now,

for who knows when it will all disappear,

and the frozen tundra

materializes right before our very own eyes again.

RF

Wandering Soul

Vagabond life.

Trust everyone

yet no one

all at once.

My soul is uneasy

while the world sleeps.

Being alone is my sanctuary,

A silent retreat.

Where I can slowly

unravel my mind

and slowly be at peace.

RF

JAMAICA —
WAS FUN
BUT NOW
I'M
PEELING.

Fool.

Silly me

always doing

the wrong thing.

Rambling and babbling .

Foolish me.

Always worrying

never truly free.

RF

Flowers & Hearts

Just as the tulips and hyacinths

flourish and thrive.

As does my loving heart,

keep increasing in size.

RF

Stalling

Stop stalling

and making excuses.

Go and do it!

No more excuses.

RF

Sleepless Nights

Sleepless nights

under the moonlight.

Stresses,

falling into a crevice.

Pitfalls, and abysses.

Tossing and turning nights,

are not what I call

a fanciful delight.

RF

Keep failing,

keep trying,

keep doing,

keep going.

Keep failing,

keep trying,

keep doing,

Keep going.

RF

Brick by Brick

Brick by brick

build yourself up.

The higher you go

the stronger you grow.

Confidence up so high,

taller than clouds in the sky.

Up so high,

No one can ever tear you down.

Up so high,

they won't even try!

RF

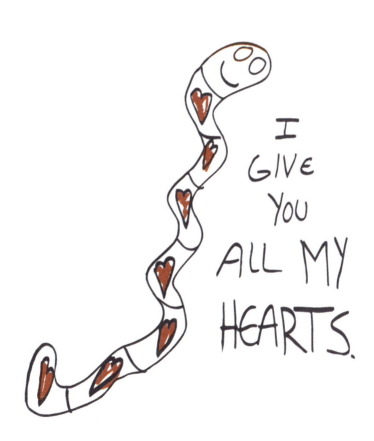

I
GIVE
YOU
ALL MY
HEARTS.

Worry

Stop worrying.

Stop dwelling on the negatives.

Do the best you can.

Even when you do that,

someone will complain,

or even mock you.

But no matter what,

Keep Shining!

Keep being you!

RF

Porcelain Boy

The world

threw you away.

Cracked and broken,

you sadly became.

Don't be angry and discouraged.

There will soon be

brighter days.

RF

Whirlwind

Falling,

Falling,

Falling,

where will we stop?

Haven't a clue darling.

Whirlwind life

blinds our sight,

blocks our roads,

where we were determined to go.

Faster,

Faster,

Faster.

Does anyone really know

what we're after?

Retreat in silence

rest in the realization

that it's okay

to not yet know our place

in this

whirlwind life.

RF

SOMETIMES PEOPLE
WON'T
LIKE
YOU.

AND THAT'S
JUST FINE

Life

Life begins.

Life ends.

Everything in between

is what we have, friends.

RF

I WEAR MASKS TO FEEL HAPPY.

Sadness comes

feelings stay.

It's hard to say,

when it will all go away.

But fear not young pal,

support is here.

Then all will be well.

RF

LOOK AT YOURSELF
WHO DO YOU WANT TO BE?
YOU DECIDE
NOT THEM

NOW GO,

BE FREE

I'M DOING BEARY BEARY GOOD.

HOW ABOUT YOU?

Drips

Drips,

drops,

on the green leaves

of this old oak tree.

Resting my head

on the mossy bark,

that's aged for a century's mark.

The ferns are unfurling,

to hear the thunderous crescendo in the sky.

Resting my head

on this old oak tree,

as the

drips,

drops,

fall from the heavenly sky.

RF

TRUST

A FRAGILE ENDEAVOR,
  BETWEEN PEOPLE
CROOKED SMILES WITH TIED HANDS
    FINGERS-CROSSED
    NO REMORSES,
ALL IS FINE ALL IS WELL
'CEPT YOU HANG ME OUT TO DRY
WHILE HOT SAND BLOWS IN MY EYES

Love

Our love is hotter than the Sun,

and deeper than the blue sea.

Laughter erupts from us,

rising higher than Mount St. Helens.

Crazy, fun filled adventure everyday.

And I wouldn't want it any other way.

RF

Noises

Too much noise

Too much distraction

Yet, we enjoy it.

It's a fatal attraction.

RF

Petals

She loves me

She loves me not.

What does it matter

When I don't know

Who I am

Or what I want.

RF

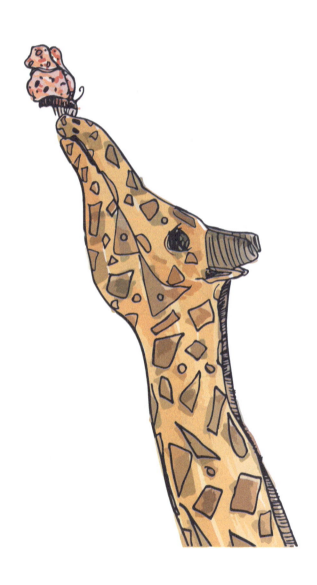

Siren's Song

The siren's song

leads me far from the shore.

Warning bells,

and lighthouse lights,

can never break my gaze.

This siren's song

is too strong,

always trapping me

below the crashing waves.

RF

Brooding Vipers

Beware of the vipers

resting in the grass,

underneath your feet.

They smile and nod

whenever you meet.

Behind closed doors

they shatter your name.

They get mad when you confront them

and say it's all part of their game.

RF

Worthy

I am not worthy

to be looked upon

with such high regard.

This title, this name

will be hard to live up too.

A father, I shall soon become.

Leader.

Head of a household

But after all,

I am only a human.

I am just...

ME

RF

Feel.

You know when you know.

It moves you.

It molds you into something else.

You can move mountains.

It will create something special,

while warming your heart.

If you don't feel that,

then move on with your life.

RF

Hold My Hand

If the world ends,

I want you there to watch,

and to hold my hand,

while I hold you tight

as the curtain falls

on our night.

RF

Rickety Rickety

Rickety rickety old bones.

Is this what my future holds?

Get out of bed... sore.

fall asleep... sore.

I mean come on,

what are these bones good for?

RF

Some Days

There are some days

where you feel like the ashes from a bon fire

burned the night before.

There are some days

where you feel like gum

stuck to the subway station floor.

There are some days

where you feel like the mistletoe

hanging in a doorway,

about to make someone's night.

There are some days

where you feel like a deer

in Autumn, staring at a swerving ca's headlight.

There are some days

where you feel out of sorts and out of place.

That doesn't define you

it's not all day, everyday.

It's just... **some days.**

RF

Whispers

Little whispers

in your head.

Steer you away

from your goals up ahead.

Delays here,

Excuses there,

Don't worry about those dreams,

they're too hard,

and far off yet.

Stay here,

and procrastinate with me instead.

RF

Left Off

Picking up,

where we last left off.

A new day is here,

to get us closer

to where we should be going,

and further from

where we have been.

RF

Beach Side

Sitting beachside,

watching the waves and the blue sky.

Abiding my time,

waiting for the high tide.

Waiting...

And waiting...

for it to carry

my stresses and doubts

far, far away from my life.

RF

Listen Closely

Listen intently

to what's beating inside your chest.

Sometimes chaos,

Sometimes heartaches and stress.

In the end,

it will never steer you wrong,

it always know what's best.

RF

Distance

Hearts apart,

right from the very start.

A distance too extreme,

"Is this really happening?

Or is it a silly dream?"

Tears, fears,

and oh so many joys,

we shared while navigating

years of uncertainty.

In the end,

it was all worth it.

The distance is now close,

and our hearts are now

attached at the seams.

RF

Hold me

Hold me

Stay with me

wait until the sun rises

Never let go

rest with me

and breathe the new dawn

Stay with me

keep me company.

RF

Simple Song

A simple song

can right the wrong.

It can help the blind,

and the lost ones to find.

Nothing else matters

except the love that you're after.

RF

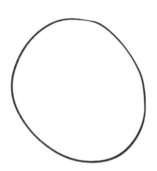

Thankful

Thanks for the friends.

Thank you for people who care.

Gracias for family.

Danka for the sunrise.

Hvala for quiet moments.

Mahalo for my doggies.

Grazie for God.

Paldies for my loving wife.

Tack for my sisters.

Go rabid math agat for my brothers.

Thankful for all y'all.

RF

www.Rexfelixx.com

27082142R00177